Long A Sound: ai

The Great Longo is a magician.
He makes long vowel words!

Add long **a** words to his magic chain.
Look at each picture.
Write the letters **ai** on the lines.
Say the word.
Write the words in the magic chain.

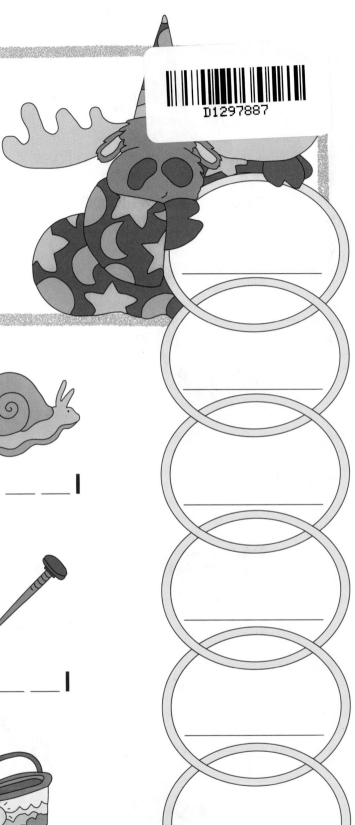

1.

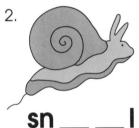

s __ __ l

2.

sn __ __ l

3.

r __ __ n

4.

n __ __ l

5.

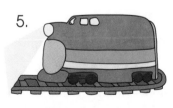

tr __ __ n

6.

p __ __ l

Long A Sound: ay

Make a long **a** playhouse! Make it with **ay** bricks!

Look at each picture.
Write the letters **ay** on the lines.
Say the word.
Write one long **a** word on each brick of the playhouse.

1.

h __ __

2.

spr __ __

3.

pl __ __

4.

j __ __

5.

tr __ __

6.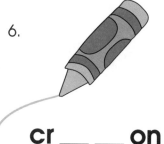

cr __ __ **on**

Long A Sound: eigh

The Great Longo had a long **a** party.
He called it the **sleigh** ride party.

Use the **eigh** words to finish the sentences.
Then read the story to find out what happened.

eight	**eighty-eight**
Neigh	**weigh**
sleigh	**Eight**

The Great Longo took __ __ __ __ __ of his friends on a

__ __ __ __ __ __ ride. "What did your horse say?" one of

his friends asked. " __ __ __ __ __ ," said Longo. Another

friend asked, "How much does your horse __ __ __ __ __ ?"

" __ __ __ __ hundred __ __ __ __ __ __ - __ __ __ __ __

pounds," said Longo.

Long A Sound: silent e

The Great Longo has a silent **e** wand!
The silent **e** wand changes words.

Many words with a long vowel sound
are spelled with a vowel, a consonant
and then **e**.

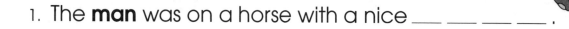

m**a**d**e**

Add an **e** to the **bold** word to make a long **a** word.
Read each sentence.

1. The **man** was on a horse with a nice ___ ___ ___ ___ .

2. He hit the **can** with his ___ ___ ___ ___ .

3. Which **hat** do you ___ ___ ___ ___ ?

4. The magician's **cap** matched his ___ ___ ___ ___ .

Long A Sound: silent e

The Great Longo is still making long **a** words with the silent **e** wand.

Write a long **a** word from each **bold** word in the sentence.
Read the sentence.

> | | |
> |---|---|
> | **pale** | **plane** |
> | **hate** | **fade** |
> | **same** | |

1. I _____ to wear this **hat**.

2. My **pal** looked sick and _____ .

3. **Sam** is on the _____ team as Joe.

4. I **plan** to fly on a _____ .

5. It is a **fad** to _____ jeans.

Long A Sound: Review

Color each long **a** word blue.
Then see what you find!

wall   far   pop   red   art   time

roar   in   say   red   to

ran   blue   play   pail   sew

cat   home   plane   sad   cane   soap

pup   eight   cake   tail   man

ten   train   ask   me   weigh   be

Long A Sound: Review

The Great Longo is on the long **a** train.

Fill the train cars with long **a** words.
Write only the long **a** words on the cars of the train.

stay	car	made	pail
hat	ask	bake	mad
ran	day	sad	bat

Long E Sound: ee

The Great Longo has a friend to help you with the long **e** sound.
His name is Buzzing Bee.

Write the correct long **e** word by each picture.
Say the word.

sheep	teeth
three	teepee
wheel	tree

1.

_____

2.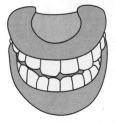

_____

3.

_____

4.

_____

5.

_____

6.

_____

Long E Sound: ea

Sometimes the letters **ea** make the long **e** sound.
Look at each picture.
Write **ea** on the lines.
Say the word.

1.

   m __ __ t

2.

   l __ __ f

3.

   s __ __ l

4.

   p __ __ nut

5.

   __ __ gle

6.

   j __ __ ns

7.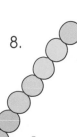

   b __ __ k

8.

   b __ __ ds

Long E Sound: ey

The Great Longo makes magic with the letters **ey**.

Write a long **e** word by adding the missing letters **ey**.
Say the word.
Draw a line from the picture to the word.

Look at all of these long **e** words made with **ey**!

1. **k** __ __

2. **monk** __ __

3. **donk** __ __

4. **hock** __ __

5. **mon** __ __

6. **turk** __ __

Long E Sound: ie, e

Help the Great Longo catch a thief!

Write the correct word by each picture.
Say the word.
Listen for the long e sound.

he   field   chief
she   shield
      cookie   thief

Long E Sound: Review

The Great Longo is hiding things!

Circle a hidden picture for each long **e** word.

cookie	key	peanut	bee	turkey
teepee	tree	wheel	leaf	penny

Long E Sound: Review

Look at each picture.
Say the word.
Circle **Yes** if the word has a long **e** sound.
Circle **No** if it does not.

1.
   thief
   Yes   No

2.
   sheep
   Yes   No

3.
   bed
   Yes   No

4.
   peach
   Yes   No

5.
   net
   Yes   No

6.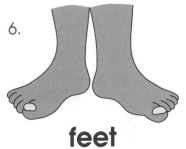
   feet
   Yes   No

7.
   men
   Yes   No

8.
   bee
   Yes   No

9.
   monkey
   Yes   No

Long I Sound: ie, y

The Great Longo makes long **i** words. He uses the
letter **y** or the letters **ie**. The Great Longo is tricky!

Read each sentence.
Then fill in the blanks with the paired words that rhyme.
Use the words in the box.

spy – sly	Why – dry
pie – tie	My – shy
Try – cry	fly – sky

1. Birds _____ in the _____ .

2. A _____ must be very _____ .

3. _____ sister is very _____ .

4. _____ not let our paintings _____ ?

5. Some _____ fell on my _____ .

6. _____ not to _____ .

Long I Sound: igh

Mighty Lion is chasing the Great Longo.

Help him get away. Write the correct word by each picture.

night	knight	light
fight	fright	right
	high	

Yeah! We made it!

15

Long I Sound: ild, ind

The Great Longo is making riddles.
The answers are long i words that end in ild or ind.

Read each sentence.
Write the correct long i word.

blind	**mind**
wild	**find**
child	**kind**

1. If you help people, you are _____ .

2. A baby is a _____ .

3. I think with my _____ .

4. If you can't see, you are _____ .

5. If you lose a toy, you try to _____ it.

6. A horse that is not tame is _____ .

Long I Sound: silent e

The Great Longo is making silent **e** words again!
This time his words have the long **i** sound.

Write a long **i** word by adding the missing **i**.
Say the word.
Draw a line from each word to its picture.

1. **d __ me**

2. **t __ me**

3. **b __ ke**

4. **k __ te**

5. **wr __ te**

6. **t __ re**

7. **f __ re**

8. **h __ ve**

Long I Sound: Review

Help the Great Longo on a long i butterfly chase!

Catch all the long i butterflies!
Color each butterfly that has a long i word on it.

Long I Sound: Review

Read each word or say each picture word.
Circle the word or picture in each row that has a long i sound.

1.

2. **nine**   **eight**   **six**

3.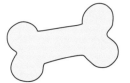

4. **gift**   **tire**   **dig**

5.

6. **baby**   **bee**   **dime**

7.

Long O Sound: oe, oa

The Great Longo makes long **o** words in many tricky ways.
Sometimes he uses **oe** to make the long **o** sound.
Sometimes he uses **oa** to make the long **o** sound.

Look at each picture.
Write in the missing letters.
Say the word.

1. t _ _

2. h _ _

3. d _ _

4. r _ _ d

5. c _ _ t

6. t _ _ st

7. b _ _ t

8. g _ _ t

9. t _ _ d

Long O Sound: o, ow, old, ost

The Great Longo is making long o sentences.
He makes the long o sound with o, ow, old, or ost.
How tricky!

Read each sentence.
Write the correct long o word.

no	**ghost**	**bowl**
go	**snow**	**Gold**
old	**crow**	

1. Get ready, get set, _____ !

2. I eat soup from a _____ .

3. White _____ fell from the sky.

4. _____ is bright and shiny.

5. Did you see a _____ on Halloween?

6. That black bird is a _____ .

7. If it's not yes, it is _____ .

8. How _____ are you?

Long O Sound: silent e

The Great Longo is lost! He wants to go home. Help him find the way.

Draw a line from the Great Longo to the first word that has the long o sound. Then draw a line to connect all of the words with the long o sound.

nose

rope

log

pop

cop

notes

pole

bone

dog

on

hole

mop

hop

rose

home

22

Long O Sound: Review

Help the Great Longo put long o words inside his giant globe!

Look at the words in the box.
Write only the words that contain the long o sound inside Longo's giant globe.
Let's go!

globe	told	rope
know	rode	note
now	row	not
goat	top	got
home	toe	lot

Long O Sound: Review

The Great Longo has a secret message waiting for you!

Color each box that has a long **o** word.

night	bump	sip	log	is
jump	cat	chip	date
rate	bowl	dog	be	hose
so	it	go	hoe	
			hat	
globe	roll	lip		he
row	old		late	
	she	ship	no	
low	lot	goat	blow	rode	toe	own
knee	hop	dip	light	hip	skate
nice	save		stop
ice	son	great	bee	not

Longo's secret message reads: _____

Long U Sound: silent e, ui, ew, ue

Draw a line from the long u word to the correct picture.
Then write the word next to the picture.

tube

1. _____

suit

2. _____

cube

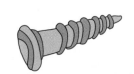

3. _____

fuel

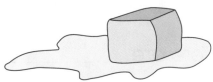

4. _____

glue

5. _____

screw

6. _____

Long U Sound: Review

Help the Great Longo make sentences with long **u** words.

Write the correct long **u** word on each line.

mew	**few**	**cute**
huge	**view**	**use**

1. If there aren't many, there are _____ .

2. I heard the kitten _____ .

3. I thought that baby was very _____ .

4. An elephant is a _____ animal.

5. Standing on a mountain, you have a nice _____ .

6. When you work with something, you _____ it.

Long Vowel Sounds: General Review

Circle the word in each row that has the same long vowel sound as the bold word.

1. **mule**   lip   fuel   hot

2. **go**   clam   nut   post

3. **chief**   milk   me   fun

4. **five**   sky   stick   gift

5. **cane**   way   fan   end

6. **leave**   step   key   miss

7. **know**   fast   float   dock

8. **rice**   mile   trick   dish

Long Vowel Sounds: General Review

Let's color Longo!

Use the sound key to color the big picture of Longo.

Long **a** – blue
Long **e** – orange
Long **i** – purple
Long **o** – brown
Long **u** – yellow

feet

beat

low

cake

go

no

pie

cube

bake

mule

mind

use

say

grow

rain

dime

eight

rake

Long Vowel Sounds: General Review

The Great Longo is playing long vowel opposites.
You can play too!

Read each word.
Write a long vowel word
that means the opposite!

take	sleep	low	sweet
dry	clean	go	white
over	cold	me	night

1. **dirty** _ _ _ _ _ _

2. **hot** _ _ _ _

3. **sour** _ _ _ _ _

4. **you** _ _

5. **black** _ _ _ _ _

6. **under** _ _ _ _

7. **day** _ _ _ _ _

8. **wake** _ _ _ _ _

9. **come** _ _

10. **give** _ _ _ _

11. **wet** _ _ _

12. **high** _ _ _

Long Vowel Sounds: General Review

Say each word.
Draw a line from the word to
the long vowel sound you hear.

1. **sheep**

2. **eight**

3. **gold**

4. **cube**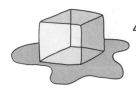

5. **try**

Long
a

Long
e

Long
i

Long
o

Long
u

6. **chief**

7. **goat**

8. **blue**

9. **wild**

10. **cane**

Long Vowel Sounds: General Review

Find all the long vowel words.
Color them green.
Then read Longo's secret message.

fog	log		had	thumb		bun		dance	
				bet		jump			pet
sit	clock		run		set			
	know			is	thief			cake
let			nice			lit	no	
	go	if		ice		hike		hill
rice			glue	pie	at		say	
cute	seen		it		rake			mean
sock				had	met			
	net	not	hit			bit	dog	
jog	has			sun	fun			mad

Longo's secret message reads: _____

Answer Key

Page 1
1. sail   4. nail
2. snail   5. train
3. rain   6. pail

Page 2
1. hay   4. jay
2. spray   5. tray
3. play   6. crayon

Page 3
1. eight   4. weigh
2. sleigh   5. Eight
3. Neigh   6. eighty-eight

Page 4
1. mane
2. cane
3. hate
4. cape

Page 5
1. hate   4. plane
2. pale   5. fade
3. same

Page 6
say, play, pail, plane, cane,
eight, cake, tail, train, weigh

Page 7
stay, made, pail, bake, day

Page 8
1. teeth   4. teepee
2. tree   5. sheep
3. wheel   6. three

Page 9
1. meat   5. eagle
2. leaf   6. jeans
3. seal   7. beak
4. peanut   8. beads

Page 10
1. key   4. hockey
2. monkey   5. money
3. donkey   6. turkey

Page 11
shield, chief, he, she,
field, cookie, thief

Page 12
Automatic fill-in.

Page 13
1. yes   5. no
2. yes   6. yes
3. no   7. no
4. yes   8. yes
9. yes

Page 14
1. fly, sky   4. Why, dry
2. spy, sly   5. pie, tie
3. My, shy   6. Try, cry

Page 15
fight, light, night, right,
knight, high, fright

Page 16
1. kind   4. blind
2. child   5. find
3. mind   6. wild

Page 17
dime, time, bike,
kite, write, tire,
fire, hive

Page 18
bike, lie, sight,
write, might, fire,
pie, wife, sky, ice

Page 19
1. fly   5. hive
2. nine   6. dime
3. bike   7. five
4. tire

Page 20
1. toe   5. coat
2. hoe   6. toast
3. doe   7. boat
4. road   8. goat
9. toad

Page 21
1. go   5. ghost
2. bowl   6. crow
3. snow   7. no
4. Gold   8. old

Page 22
nose, rope, pole, notes,
bone, hole, rose, home

Page 23
globe, told, rope, know,
rode, note, row, goat,
home, toe

Page 24
globe, low, row, bowl, so, roll,
goat, go, old, blow, hoe, no,
rode, hose, toe, own, **(HELLO)**

Page 25
1. glue   4. fuel
2. cube   5. suit
3. screw   6. tube

Page 26
1. few   4. huge
2. mew   5. view
3. cute   6. use

Page 27
1. fuel   5. way
2. post   6. key
3. me   7. float
4. sky   8. mile

Page 28
Automatic fill-in.

Page 29
1. clean   7. night
2. cold   8. sleep
3. sweet   9. go
4. me   10. take
5. white   11. dry
6. over   12. low

Page 30
1. long e   6. long e
2. long a   7. long o
3. long o   8. long u
4. long u   9. long i
5. long i   10. long a

Page 31
rice, cute, know, go, seen,
nice, glue, pie, ice, thief,
rake, hike, no, say, mean,
cake, **(LONGO)**